The Trouble with Tadpoles
A First Look at the Life Cycle of a Frog

by Sam Godwin   illustrated by Simone Abel

Thanks to our reading adviser:

Susan Kesselring, M.A., Literacy Educator
Rosemount-Apple Valley-Eagan (Minnesota) School District

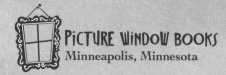

PICTURE WINDOW BOOKS
Minneapolis, Minnesota

First American edition published in 2005 by
Picture Window Books
5115 Excelsior Boulevard
Suite 232
Minneapolis, MN 55416
877-845-8392
www.picturewindowbooks.com

First published in Great Britain in 1999 by Macdonald Young Books,
an imprint of Wayland Publishers Ltd.
Published in 2001 by Hodder Wayland, Hodder Children's Books
A division of Hodder Headline Limited
338 Euston Road
London NW1 3BH

Text copyright © Sam Godwin
Illustrations copyright © Simone Abel

Printed in the United States of America.

Library of Congress Cataloging-in-Publication Data
Godwin, Sam.
The trouble with tadpoles : a first look at the life cycle of a frog/ by
Sam Godwin ; illustrated by Simone Abel.
p. cm.—(First look : science)
ISBN 1-4048-0654-7 (hardcover)
1. Frogs—Life cycles—Juvenile literature. 2. Tadpoles—Juvenile
literature. I. Abel, Simone, ill. II. Title. III. Series.
QL668.E2G579 2004
597.8'139—dc22   2004007321

For Yan – SG
For Joyce and Peter with love – SA

3

It's spring, and a wiggly tadpole swims around the pond.

Where did the tadpole come from?

5

A tadpole starts life inside a tiny egg.

The eggs are called frog spawn. They're wrapped in a special kind of jelly.

Did someone
say jelly?
Yum, yum.

Lots of these eggs float together in the weeds.

The egg slowly hatches, and a tiny tadpole wiggles into the water.

Tadpoles—yum!

It hides in the weeds where it feels safe.

Leave that tadpole alone, you big bully!

It has gills to help it breathe in water like a fish.

11

Hey, those tadpole legs look a bit like yours. I wonder why?

Then, very slowly, something amazing happens.

The tadpole starts to grow two legs.

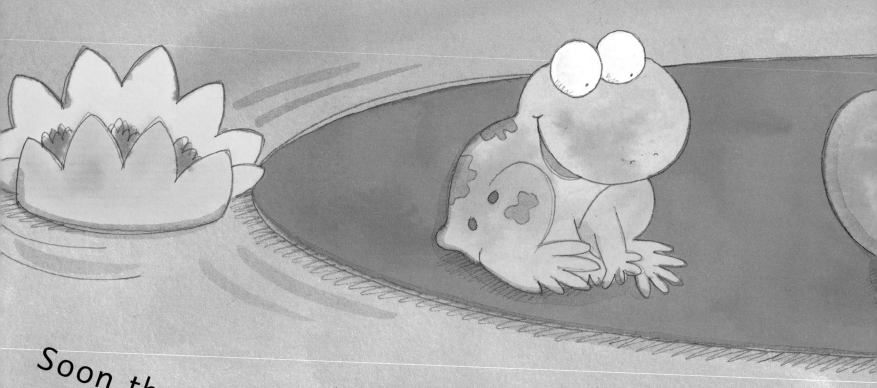

Soon the tadpole starts to grow two front legs.

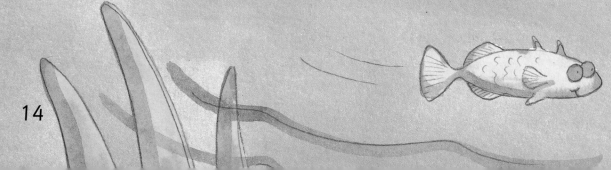

14

The tadpole has changed inside, too—it has grown lungs and can breathe on land, just like us.

Its tail begins to get smaller and smaller.

At last, the tadpole is not a tadpole anymore.

16

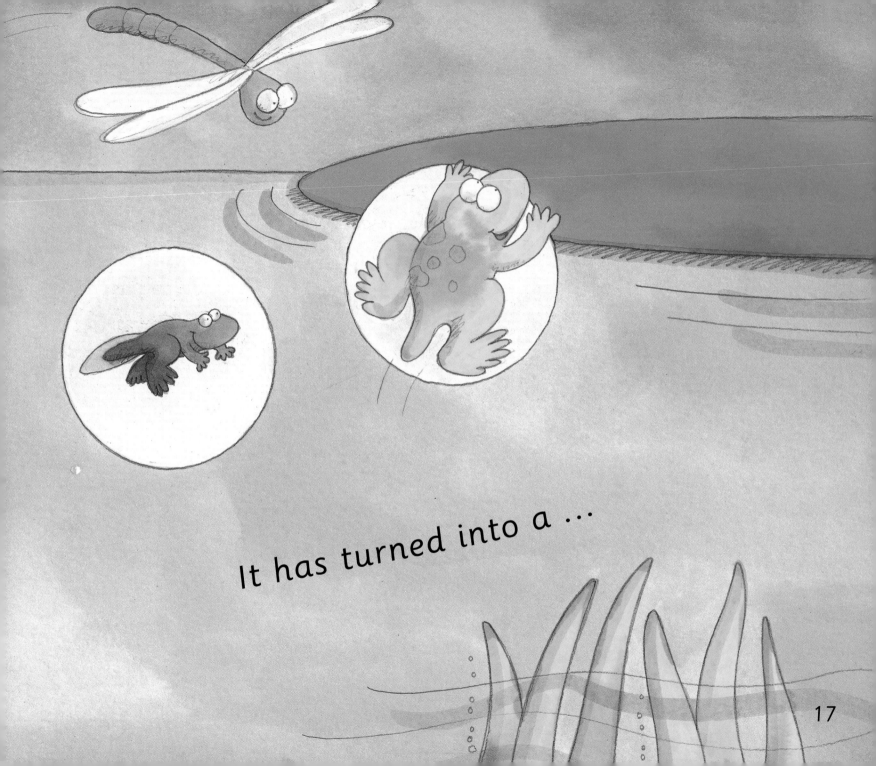

It has turned into a ...

FROG!

18

19

The baby frog grows fast. It learns to croak,

jump, and catch flies with its long tongue.

but they always stay close to water.

In spring, grown-up frogs return to the pond.

How many eggs does a mommy lay?

It could be as many as 5,000. Amazing, huh?

The mommy frogs lay spawn in the weeds.

25

In no time at all, the spawn hatches and

new tadpoles are born.

The Frog Life Cycle

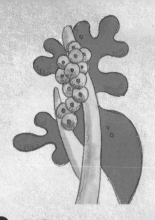

1 Frogs lay spawn in the weeds.

2 A baby tadpole hatches out of each egg and clings to the weeds.

9 Adult frogs are ready to lay more spawn.

8 The frog's tail disappears completely.

28

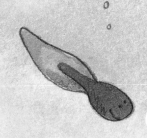

3 The tadpole has outside gills like a fish. After a few days, it starts to feed on weeds.

4 The tadpole loses its outside gills. It now has gills inside its head.

5 The tadpole starts to grow back legs. It also starts to develop lungs.

7 The tadpole's lungs are fully grown, so it can breathe on land.

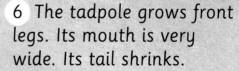

6 The tadpole grows front legs. Its mouth is very wide. Its tail shrinks.

Useful Words

Croak
The low, echoey sound that some frogs make.

Frog Spawn
A mass of frog's eggs or tiny baby tadpoles wrapped in a layer of jelly. This jelly protects and provides food for them.

Gills
The part of a fish or tadpole that helps it to breathe under water. They look like small wings and can be seen on either side of a tadpole's head.

Hatch
When a baby bird or fish wiggles out of the egg in which it started life.

Lungs
The part of animals and humans that helps them to breathe out of water. Lungs cannot be seen because they are inside the body, usually in the chest.

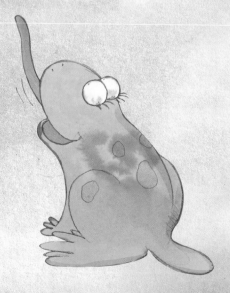

Fun Facts

Frogs don't need to drink because they absorb water through their skin.

Most frogs can jump more than 20 times their own body length.

A group of frogs is called an army of frogs.

Some frogs adjust the color of their skin to blend in with their surroundings.

To Learn More

At the Library

Trumbauer, Lisa. *The Life Cycle of a Frog.* Mankato, Minn.: Pebble Books, 2002.

Wallace, Karen. *Tale of a Tadpole.* New York: Dorling Kindersley Publishing, 1998.

Zoehfeld, Kathleen Weidner. *From Tadpole to Frog.* New York: Scholastic, 2002.

On the Web

FactHound offers a safe, fun way to find Web sites related to this book. All of the sites on FactHound have been researched by our staff. *www.facthound.com*

1. Visit the FactHound home page.
2. Enter a search word related to this book, or type in this special code:1404806547.
3. Click the FETCH IT button.

Your trusty FactHound will fetch the best Web sites for you!

Index

eggs, 6, 7, 8, 24, 28

frog spawn, 6, 25, 26, 28, 30

gills, 11, 29, 30

hatch, 8, 26, 28, 30

legs, 12, 13, 14, 29

lungs, 15, 29, 30

pond, 4, 24

tail, 15, 28, 29

weeds, 7, 9, 10, 25, 28, 29

Look for all the books in this series:

A Seed in Need
A First Look at the Plant Cycle

And Everyone Shouted, "Pull!"
A First Look at Forces of Motion

From Little Acorns ...
A First Look at the Life Cycle of a Tree

Paint a Sun in the Sky
A First Look at the Seasons

Take a Walk on a Rainbow
A First Look at Color

The Case of the Missing Caterpillar
A First Look at the Life Cycle of a Butterfly

The Drop Goes Plop
A First Look at the Water Cycle

The Hen Can't Help It
A First Look at the Life Cycle of a Chicken

The Trouble with Tadpoles
A First Look at the Life Cycle of a Frog